BLESSED

A 30-DAY DEVOTIONAL
TO ENCOURAGE YOUR LIFE

Mike Sternad

BLESSED
A 30-DAY DEVOTIONAL TO ENCOURAGE YOUR LIFE

By Mike Sternad

Published by Contented Life Publishing

Mailing Address: 312 T Schillinger Rd. S,
Mobile, Alabama 36608

Website: www.calvarychapelmobile.com
Email: mikesternad@gmail.com

Edited by Miriam Rogers
Cover Design by Ashley Garcia
Interior Design by Ulrika Towgood

ISBN 978-0-578-59419-4

Printed in the United States of America

This book is dedicated to
my beautiful wife and my two amazing daughters.
You bring me so much joy in this life.
I am a blessed husband and father.

TABLE OF CONTENTS

TABLE OF CONTENTS (Continued)

INTRODUCTION

> *"Blessed is the man who walks not in the counsel of the ungodly, nor stands in the path of sinners, nor sits in the seat of the scornful; but his delight is in the law of the LORD, and in His law he meditates day and night. He shall be like a tree planted by the rivers of water, that brings forth its fruit in its season, whose leaf also shall not wither; and whatever he does shall prosper."* (Psalm 1:1-3)

To be a believer in Jesus Christ is an absolute blessing. *Blessed* means *Oh, how happy*. In Christ we have all the spiritual riches we could ever desire. To be blessed is the result of actively walking with the Lord on a daily basis. The world's ways are quickly sliding down a sad and slippery slope. It is such a blessing to be living for the Lord and shining as lights for Him in this dark and damaged world. Oftentimes as believers we ask God for blessings without realizing that we are blessed already—we are saved, sealed and set for heaven. Not only will the future be a blessing, but we are also blessed by the past and what we've been through. God turns our past mistakes and trials and uses them as a testimony to encourage others in the Lord. He endows us with amazing gifts in the present. Being Christians means we believe and accept Christ as Savior, and if we are never given anything in addition to Him, we still remain super blessed. Jesus is enough. It is He we look to and are saved through (John 14:6). If you are a believer, you are blessed.

"Blessed be the God and Father of our Lord Jesus Christ, who has blessed us with every spiritual blessing in the heavenly places in Christ." (Ephesians 1:3)

This devotional is all about the blessings that fall from above. It's about realizing you are not in want (Psalm 23), but you are satisfied, fulfilled and free in Christ. You are blessed so abundantly by God that a short devotional barely scratches the surface of your abundant blessings from God. This devotional was written as a reminder of how your Redeemer has rained down so many gifts that you can't help but be overwhelmed in a good way. Christians understand the darkening world, but they also understand the bright outcome of the future. Believers should be the most optimistic people on this earth. We not only revel in what God has given us, we are also blessed in order to bless others by sharing the gospel with them. Realize you are blessed from above and you have the great privilege to share those blessings with those whom God places in your path. Look up to the Lord before you look ahead to the world. Even in adversity and affliction remember that God has given you every spiritual blessing to comfort you and get you through every single situation that you face.

Mike Sternad
Pastor, Calvary Chapel Mobile, Alabama

DAY 1

BEYOND BLESSED

"For I know the thoughts that I think toward you, says the LORD, thoughts of peace and not of evil, to give you a future and a hope. Then you will call upon Me and go and pray to Me, and I will listen to you." (Jeremiah 29:11-12)

God absolutely loves you. He sees you through the lens of love. God's thoughts toward you are not mean, wrathful, evil or angry; they are of complete peace.

It's a complete blessing to realize the view God has of His children. We can be joyful because His promises are valid despite our imperfections. We are blessed because the Father has a clear-cut calling for each of us—a future that is full of purpose. Blessings from God come when we simply obey His will for our lives. As we stay faithful in those little things, God will continue to guide and direct us on the path He is paving for us. We can be completely happy because God leads us out of His love for us.

The Father blesses us with a future that is full of purpose.

What a blessing to know God hears every single one of our prayers. Unlike a person who has a hard time listening, God is attentive to our prayers. He listens. He hears us and He responds to us in various ways. Sometimes in a still small voice, sometimes through

His Word, sometimes through sermons we hear, sometimes through situations, and sometimes through other people. God, who created the universe, hears our seemingly small personal prayers. What a blessing beyond comprehension! Yet, the reality that God hears us can radically transform our prayer life and cause a commitment to prayer that is unstoppable. We are blessed because we have open communication with our Lord!

Today, know that the Lord thinks good thoughts toward you. Know that the Lord loves you so much that He has a future and a hope planned out for you. Know that the God of the universe will always have time to hear and respond to your prayers, no matter how small and insignificant you think they are. All these things demonstrate the true love God has for you. Find joy in the fact that you are beyond blessed.

DAY 2

BLESSED FROM ABOVE

"My God shall supply all your need according to His riches in glory by Christ Jesus." (Philippians 4:19)

Our God is so good that He blessed us by sending His Son to live, die, and rise again so we could be set free. Through Christ we are saved and set apart to live our lives as an offering to God. What a joy to know that God doesn't withhold beautiful blessings, but freely lavishes them on us.

Our spiritual supply will remain full as we follow the Lord. We will lack nothing in this temporary timeframe when it comes to heavenly riches. We are so rich in Christ that no trial can tear us down; no storms in life can wash us away from God—because God gives us an eternal perspective.

> God gives us all the spiritual blessings we need to navigate through this sin-ridden world.

The fact that Paul wrote *My God* shows we can have personal interaction with the infinite God. The Lord is not hidden away in some undisclosed location, withdrawn and far away from humanity. As we draw near to Him, He will draw near to us (James 4:8). God awaits the ones who would pursue Him fully and constantly. The Lord desires to have a close and tight-knit relationship with us. May we keep our eyes focused on Him, our hearts bent toward Him, and our lives aligned with His will. The result of these proactive actions will be bountiful blessings. Where God locationally guides us, God will graciously provide for us. Be blessed by the fact that we have every single spiritual blessing in Christ Jesus.

Today, remember that God's spiritual blessings toward you are bountiful. If you know and have accepted Jesus, then you are saved, redeemed and forgiven—you are blessed from above. He has equipped you with everything you need to be abundantly joyful. You don't have to think about all that you lack as a believer—you lack nothing! Think about all that God has blessed you with from above. When you realize God's plentiful blessings, your heart will be full, and your soul will be secure. There is no greater blessing than that!

TRUST GOD

"Oh, taste and see that the LORD is good; blessed is the man who trusts in Him!" (Psalm 34:8)

God is good all the time. When our circumstances seem less than favorable, God is good. When our lives are filled with conflicts that seem never-ending, God is still good. When our day does not go according to plan, God is still good. When our present circumstances seem to be filled with problems, God is still good. When the future seems to fall through, God is still good. We can be 100 percent sure that the Lord is good through every situation because we know Him, walk with Him, and have a personal relationship with Him. As we seek God, we are blessed by His goodness and His great love for us.

We will see that the Lord is good as we set our eyes upon Him and seek to know Him more intimately. We will taste that the Lord is good and respond by simply falling at His feet and feeding off of His goodness. What a comfort and blessing to know that God is good no matter what lies ahead of us.

As we seek God we are blessed by His goodness.

Everyone wants to be happy, to have joy in this life. All of humanity seeks fulfillment. What action do we need to take in order to be fulfilled and joyful? The answer to the satisfied life is to simply trust in God!

As we stick close to the Lord, we are saying yes to surrendering to Him. When we trust in our Lord, we realize how incredibly good He is, and the result will be abundant and beautiful joy. The natural progression that follows trusting the Lord is a heart of worship and adoration. What a blessing to simply respond to the Lord by praising Him for His goodness. He knows exactly what we need for every situation.

Today, trust God with your whole heart. Know that He is good. He is in control of your life and will never lead you astray. You can find happiness by holding on to the One who will always love you. You can be satisfied by God as you simply set your affections upon Him. You will be fulfilled and content as you daily depend upon Him through it all.

GOD'S BLESSINGS

"Blessed is he who considers the poor; the LORD will deliver him in time of trouble." (Psalm 41:1)

Joy comes from helping those who are in need. We were made to help others. We were created to consider those whose conflicted circumstances have led to their difficulty and despondency. Our secondary mission is to help materially.

Our primary mission is to share the good news of Jesus Christ. We have the privilege of passing along truth that is transformative. We have what humanity desperately needs—news that can tear apart any trial. Consider the poor by first paying attention to them. Pray for them, encourage them in God's Word, give them Jesus, and leave them with Jesus. As we reach out to those in need, God will do a work through us. All we have to do is be available and pray for discernment on whom to reach out to. God can help the most helpless person, and He can use us to do so. What a complete blessing.

> We are blessed to share the news that can tear apart any trial.

We are the Lord's messengers, but God is the soul deliverer. The Lord is the One who rescues and resuscitates those who are helpless. The Lord is the lifeguard who jumps in the water and saves those who are drowning. We simply steer the boat to the location of the people who are barely treading water. God's heart is to help; may our hearts line up with His. May we let God use us to be truth tellers to those who are suffering major trials.

Today, consider the helpless and hopeless. God wants to use you to reach out to those who are broken and battered. God wants to use you to relay your testimony to those who are falling apart—to be a light to the person who feels stuck in his or her situation and is crying out for help. Pray against passivity and ask God to annihilate your inhibitions as you pass along the good news of Jesus Christ. You deliver the message; God will deliver the soul. It's not a burden to help—it's a blessing. The result of reaching out to the helpless will be God's blessings poured abundantly into your heart.

DAY 5

ABSOLUTE BLESSING

"His lord said to him, 'Well done, good and faithful servant; you were faithful over a few things, I will make you ruler over many things. Enter into the joy of your lord.'" (Matthew 25:21)

Our goal in this life is to live for God in the location where He has us, in the present moment. It is an absolute blessing to simply serve the Lord. You and I have the privilege of waking up every morning and being available to live a faith-filled life for God's glory. We have the opportunity to be faithful in all that we do and say. And when we are consistently faithful in the small things, the Lord will bless us with more tasks and missions that we can be faithful in. When we give our all for the Lord, we are blessed because God is blessed.

The apostle Paul's aim in life was to please God. The Lord is who we live for and aim to please. When God calls us to something, and we answer that calling and follow Him every step of the way, we are blessing God! To make God's heart happy is the greatest blessing we could ever ask for. To serve the Lord with all that's within us is an amazing privilege.

To be faithful fills us with joy.

As believers, we have much to look forward to. We get to live our lives on this earth for God, and when our earthly race is over, we get to hear the Lord say, "Well done." One day in the future we will have unhindered and unbridled joy in heaven. The future is bright for those who remain faithful. May we continue to live a surrendered life and joyfully tread down the path that God has paved for us. Life is too short to be an unfaithful and inconsistent child of God. We don't want to look back and be filled with regret because we refused to be faithful in all that God has entrusted to us.

Today, live to please the Lord. May your motivation be to please the Lord. May you continue to be faithful with what is in front of you. May you produce fruit where you are planted and thrive where the Lord has you at this very moment. Know that the Lord has you in your present location because He wants to use you greatly. Keep your eyes on the Lord and your hand to the plow. Remember that it's not a burden to serve the Lord, it is an absolute blessing.

DAY 6

STAY CONNECTED

"Blessed are those who keep His testimonies, who seek Him with the whole heart!" (Psalm 119:2)

We are blessed to have the whole counsel of God. We have the privilege of digging into the Bible and doing what it says. When we keep the Lord's testimonies, we are being obedient to Him. The word *obedience* has come to have very negative connotations today. Yet obedience to our God leads to entrance into the full and fruitful will of God.

The most fulfilling life is a life that is fully surrendered to God. Blessings abound as we have the privilege to adhere to the Holy Spirit-inspired Word of God. Following God's Word doesn't mean we strive for perfection; it means freedom to follow what the Lord has outlined for us. As the Lord has our best interest in mind, being obedient to God will keep us on the right path. We get a glimpse into God's heart and a written record of God's ways that we are blessed to adhere to.

Joy comes from embracing and enacting God's Word.

When the core of who we are seeks after and collides with the Creator of the universe, blessings abound. Pursue the Lord and lay procrastination aside. Seek God and daily die to self to get out of God's way and into His will. When we lay down our surface level dreams and fix our eyes on God's perfect plans, there's no question that blessings will follow. Continue to seek Him and be led by the testimonies He has given in His Word. The result of seeking God with our whole heart is blessings from above.

Today, be blessed by bravely seeking the Lord with your very being. Keep His Word but do not condemn yourself. Follow His Word but do not get in the way of His will. Stay connected to the Scriptures and saturate yourself in God's Word constantly and consistently. There is no need to get bogged down by this world, but every reason to be blessed by God's Word.

DAY 7

BLEAKNESS TO BLESSINGS

"And God is able to make all grace abound toward you, that you, always having all sufficiency in all things, may have an abundance for every good work." (2 Corinthians 9:8)

God's grace is a tremendous blessing. The Lord's unmerited favor helps us to flourish in the faith completely unhindered. We deserve nothing good, yet God gives us every spiritual blessing. We are forgiven, free and relieved of the drudgery of working for rewards. We can never earn an ounce of grace, nor can we ever work for a portion of grace and there's no way we can strive for God's grace.

The Lord makes grace abound toward people who are in desperate need of His grace. Condemnation has no place in the Christian life. There is *no* condemnation in Christ—not now, not ever (Romans 8:1). God's grace is gargantuan and will destroy any deep condemnation that you have or will ever face. We are free because of God's great grace that engulfs every hint of self-condemnation.

God's grace extends from heaven to earth.

When Paul was suffering from affliction, Jesus said to him, "My grace is sufficient for you, for My strength is made perfect in weakness" (2 Corinthians 12:9). Despite the obstacles we face and the trials that try to stop us, we can move forward because of God's amazing grace. To accomplish work for our almighty God, it's imperative that we understand His grace will not go away. His grace is towering above us driving God's sufficiency toward us. We are bombarded with blessings because of God's great favor. Embrace God's grace every day and watch Him transform your outlook from bleakness to blessings.

Today, know that God's grace is aimed directly at your heart. Let His grace engulf any and all guilt you are holding on to. Allow God's grace to give you the strength to go all out for the Lord. God's grace is the fuel that will fill your faith and fortify your connection with your Creator.

DAY 8

HOLD ON

"God shall bless us, and all the ends of the earth shall fear Him." (Psalm 67:7)

God is a giver. There is no way that we can outgive the Lord. God is the source of every good gift that we have ever received. Not only has God blessed us in the past, He will bless us in the future. When our focus is on the eternal, we can be extremely expectant that God will supply everything we need, and more.

There are times when we don't know how we would make it through; moments when it feels like we are at our end, seasons where it seems like all we know is suffering. Even in those unsure times, God will make sure that we are supernaturally provided for. There is no need to doubt the Lord will do a miracle in those situations that we see as impossible. Those moments when things seem so strenuous are the very moments our trust in the Lord needs to soar. We must believe that God is our treasure and He will give us all we need to survive and thrive in this life.

Blessings bombard us as believers.

Grateful hearts result from the actions of our gracious Father. As the Lord rains down blessings from above, we receive those blessings and then respond to the Lord in adoration. When we experience the Lord's miraculous provision in our own lives, we will respond in joyful worship. When we know without a shadow of a doubt that God has come through once again, we will be reminded that He always comes through. "And all the ends of the earth shall fear Him." Fearing God means we truly trust that He is in complete control of our situations from season to season.

Today, remember that God will come through and provide for you. There is no need to doubt. There's no need to be down. As you depend upon the Lord, blessings will flow from heaven to your heart. God knows what you need; He sees your struggle. Even in your brokenness God will bless you and comfort you as you simply hold on to the Most High. Trust Him in your trials.

GOD FAVORS YOU

"For the LORD takes pleasure in His people;
He will beautify the humble with salvation."
(Psalm 149:4)

God is blessed by us. We don't often think in those terms; we usually think in terms of how extremely blessed we are by the Lord. Yet God takes pleasure in His people. Yes, we are incredibly imperfect, and we make many mistakes, but this fact never diminishes God's favor upon us. God's grace makes it possible for Him to love us no matter what. He takes pleasure in us as we live for His purposes. When we truly realize that the Lord takes pleasure in His people, we will finally have the right view and perspective of God. Our almighty God is not a wrathful dictator waiting to pounce on us. Even with all of our perceived imperfections, we are still God's work of art.

God is blessed as we live to bless Him.

Salvation is a beautiful truth. Those who believe and accept the gospel are saved. Those who humble themselves are saved and set for a future in heaven. Those who confess with their mouth and believe in their heart that Jesus died and rose again are saved (Romans 10:9). Sincerely humbling ourselves before the Lord is one of the first steps to salvation.

Those who are humble possess the right attitude to be saved since they are not focused on themselves. They put the Lord first, others second, and themselves last. The Bible makes it clear that God doesn't humble us, but that we are to humble ourselves. God is extremely pleased with those who have selfless hearts. God exalts His children not because of achievement or earthly success, but because their hearts are humble. Humility is a step toward salvation—this is a beautiful truth that sets us on the path of pleasing the Lord.

Today, may your countenance be lifted as you realize the Lord is pleased with you. Even with all your faults God favors you. You are a blessing to the Lord as you continually humble your heart and hold onto Him. He takes pleasure in you, not because you've done something to earn it, but because He is full of grace and mercy. May this truth kill any condemnation you are harboring and fill you with complete peace.

DAY 10

OVERWHELMINGLY BLESSED

"Salvation belongs to the LORD. Your blessing is upon Your people." (Psalm 3:8)

We cannot save ourselves. No matter how hard we try, there is no way we can make our way to heaven without the Lord being involved. When a person is saved it is by God's grace through faith (Ephesians 2:8-9) —not a result of a person working extra hard and constantly striving. We are blessed to be saved because the Lord entered the atmosphere of our lives. We are blessed because God in His grace reached down and saved us from drowning. Salvation is a sweet blessing from the Savior of the world. May we never take salvation for granted; instead, let us find joy that the Lord intervened in our life circumstances. He divinely interrupted our selfish plans and reverted our goal from selfish living to selflessly dying to our flesh. The Lord changed our goal from following our dreams to fulfilling His purposes.

> Salvation is the result of our holy God reaching down to sinful humanity and radically changing our hearts.

God's blessings are upon those who are His. The Lord desires none to perish, yet those who reject the truth will be separated from God when these bodies wear out. The reality is we are all going to face the Lord when our earthly tents fail. If we aren't saved and living for Jesus here on this earth, then we won't be with Him in eternity. This truth should wake us up to the fact that many are lost and need the directional map to go from stranded to saved. It should help us to realize we need to relay the truth to a broken and torn apart world. This earth and the way it's going is not good. It continues to grow darker and darker. May we have eyes to see people the way the Lord sees them, lost and needing to be found.

Today, if you are a child of God, count yourself overwhelmingly blessed. Salvation belongs to the Lord and you belong to Him. Don't take for granted that you are saved. May your heart soar with joy knowing He has pursued you, saved you, sealed you, and is setting up your eternal home in heaven. Your future in heaven will lack any sadness and sorrow because the Lord will be right there with you.

DAY 11

BELIEVE GOD

> *"Jesus said to him, 'Thomas, because you have seen Me, you have believed. Blessed are those who have not seen and yet have believed.'"*
> (John 20:29)

We are blessed by simply believing. Thomas had a hard time believing from the onset. It took time to test the truth, to make sure what he was seeing was real. In life we often need to see to believe. We won't make decisions until we know the truth and see tangible results. We will not take a step until we know something is sure. Although there is wisdom in that way of thinking, Jesus tells us what true faith leading to happiness really is.

Happiness comes from hiking through this life following God as our trail guide. He is working behind the scenes. He is the director, orchestrating this movie that is our life. Our story has a beginning, middle and ending. We cannot see the full novel, but we do believe that God is the Author and each believer ends up with Him at the end of the story.

> True faith is believing in the spiritual side of life without seeing every single detail.

It's not that we are to have unthinking blind faith. That's ridiculous and unbiblical. Having faith means we forge ahead following the Lord even when we don't see the whole outcome and ending. Much of our doubt may stem from being unsure because we don't have every single duck in a row. Jesus made it clear that having faith isn't having all the visual details in everything we do. Having faith is a deep dependency upon Him knowing He has it all planned out. All we have to do is follow Him and trust that He knows where we need to go.

The spiritual realm is real, and we need to be aware of those unseen forces that are good and bad, dark and light. When we are aware of the fact that the spiritual not only exists but has a major influence on our lives, we will change what we do and the way we live. It is a blessing to know that the Lord is working as we walk by faith through this God-given life.

Today, be blessed by the fact that God is working in your life. Your sight can only take you so far, but walking by faith leads to the adventure that God has for you. Walking by faith means you believe God is doing great things in your life, even if all of them haven't happened yet. He is working it all out for your good (Romans 8:28). His plan for your life is being accomplished even if you don't know all the details. Let the Lord take control, and willingly walk by faith. You will be blessed as you solely depend upon the Lord's plan for your life. He has a future for you, and it's amazing.

DAY 12

ETERNAL INHERITANCE

"Blessed is the nation whose God is the LORD, the people He has chosen as His own inheritance."
(Psalm 33:12)

The key to happiness stems from our relationship with the Lord. When someone knows the Lord and follows Him passionately, they are blessed and want to share their blessings. We don't share the Lord with other people because we have to; we share the Lord because we have been transformed by Him and we desire to pass on the truth that God can do radical work. It's a privilege to preach. It's a blessing to be a beacon of light. It's an honor to herald the good news. To see whole families or groups of friends affected by the gospel is one of the best blessings ever. There's nothing like seeing cities and counties transformed by the power of God.

How amazing when a nation sets the Lord as its number one priority. In 1 Samuel the Israelites had been letting the Lord lead. Yet, they became restless and demanded a human leader like the other nations. Because of their hard hearts and stubborn ways, God allowed the people to elect a human leader. As a result, Saul became the first king of Israel. His rule started off well, but definitely didn't end well. People are imperfect and make mistakes. The best leader can end up leading people down the wrong path.

> When God is the One who leads us, we are in a solid spiritual state.

What a blessing to know we've inherited riches that far surpass any earthly thing. As precious children of the Lord we have an eternal inheritance. We are chosen by God to inherit all the eternal riches from heaven above. And God is pleased with those who take directives from Him; when His people walk in the purposes He has for them. When we simply follow God's lead, we will not get lost. We will be found, and we will see profound spiritual progress.

Today, glory in the fact that God is your Lord. He is who leads you in this life. You have a heavenly inheritance as you have been chosen by Him. Let the fact that you have a loving relationship with God overwhelm you to such an extent that you can't help but give testimony of your transformation. Remember that you are extremely blessed because of your eternal inheritance.

STRENGTH AND PEACE

"The LORD will give strength to His people; the LORD will bless His people with peace."
(Psalm 29:11)

What a blessing to be endowed with strength from above. We can strive for every ounce of earthly strength and still be left weak and helpless. Sometimes we have nothing left because we attempt to live life without His strength. There are moments where our walk with the Lord is waning and we feel defeated. Those are the very moments we need to stop striving in our own strength and start seeking God's strength. The Lord can endow us with great strength as we simply sit at His feet and depend upon Him. A small portion of the Lord's strength can get us through the biggest trials.

Knowing that He is the source of strength we need in this life is super comforting.

The Lord blesses His people with amazingly authentic peace. Often people are in a place where technically, they should have complete peace. Circumstances line up and things are going well. Yet, their hearts are in a state of turmoil and stress. They still feel anxious and alone, uneasy and unsteady. They wonder why they have no peace in the midst of success. The problem is that people think peace comes from many different places when in reality there is only one source of peace. Peace does not originate from circumstances, situations or locations. Peace isn't the result of winning at worldly pursuits. Peace is produced by the Lord and ingrained in His people whenever and wherever we are. We have peace from the Lord though tribulation threatens to tear us apart. Remember to call upon the Lord and ask Him to fill your heart with peace in the middle of your biggest problem.

Today, you have the blessing of possessing complete peace from the Peace-giver (John 14:27). Maybe you are facing turmoil and your circumstances are shaky and unsure. Maybe you are in a storm and find it hard to remain steady and stable. Maybe you feel weak, and therefore have no relief or rest. What will remedy all these afflictions is to remember that the Lord is who will give you strength and peace. You will gain peace as you look to God.

SPIRITUAL BLESSING

"But he who looks into the perfect law of liberty and continues in it, and is not a forgetful hearer but a doer of the work, this one will be blessed in what he does." (James 1:25)

Following God's Word leads to abundant blessings. One of the greatest actions we can take as believers is continuing in His Word on a daily basis. Reading God's Word shouldn't be an occasional occurrence; it should be a continual progression. When we continue in God's Word, we are blessed to get to know His heart and His ways.

We will remember God's Word by regularly reading it—not only reading but heeding it as well. Not only reading but living and acting it out. We can keep from forgetting God's Word by delving in the truths that call us to action. We'll be happy as we hear God's Word and take action in the God-given plan He has for us. God is perfect, and as we adhere to His perfect Word, we will be on His purposeful path for us.

Hearing and heeding God's Word result in profound spiritual progress.

Every time we put in work by reading God's Word, it leads to bountiful blessings. If we remain obedient, we are in God's will. If we are in God's will, then everything we do will be led by the Lord and will lead to joy. Every day we will have great opportunities to be used by the Lord as we are willing to hear His calling, align ourselves with His Word, and respond to that calling. The Lord's purpose in this life is that we profess the absolute truth contained in the Bible, the book that is God-breathed.

Today, continue in God's Word and put into practice what He says. You are made to fulfill God's will. You are equipped with every spiritual blessing to put into place God's purposes for you. Look to the Lord by looking into His Word. As God impresses His calling upon your heart, act on your calling—don't let it slowly die within you. Be proactive for your almighty God! Stay in His Word, discover His ways, and work them out in your life. You will be blessed by living out the plan God has for you.

DAY 15

BURDENS INTO BLESSINGS

"Blessed is the man who trusts in the LORD, and whose hope is the LORD." (Jeremiah 17:7)

Trusting in the Lord is a blessing that cannot be breached. When we trust in God, no one can break that trust or get between us and the Lord. Trusting God will alter our daily outlook. Trusting God will put us on the street of God's sovereignty. Trusting God will bridge the gap from our hearts to His. Trusting God allows us to lay on the gurney in weakness, allowing God in His strength to pull us along His desired path. Traversing the opposite way of our Lord's path will cause separation from His perfect will for us.

As we place our faith in our Provider, we surrender ourselves to His authority, and in so doing we will be able to trek through any trial with a heart that is full. God knows what's best for us in every single real-time situation. We can fully trust that the Lord will lead us in love. He always desires the best for us. Give up the fight, raise the white flag of surrender, and let God lead.

God can take deep heartache and turn it into daily hope.

Blessed is the one who hangs on tightly to the hope from heaven. God knows when we desperately need uplifting encouragement. He unlocks the vault of hope and helps believers see that burdens can easily revert to blessings as our eyes gaze upon God. When hope pervades our outlook, it interrupts our hardships, and the result will be freedom and relief. God will bring rest as a result of hurling hope into our hearts.

Today, you can be blessed by simply trusting the Lord and gripping onto the hope that you have in Him. Hope emanates from a heart that has already been filled by your Father. You will be at complete rest when you hope in the Lord, not the world. Today, remember how blessed you are—you have hope when you have the Lord. Call upon Him for enough hope to turn burdens into blessings. You have a multitude of blessings that come from simply trusting the God who made the heavens and the earth. If you lack hope, hold onto the Lord. He will never let you down.

KNOWING THE LORD

"And the LORD restored Job's losses when he prayed for his friends. Indeed the LORD gave Job twice as much as he had before." (Job 42:10)

Difficulties do not diminish God's blessings toward us. Job went through so much affliction that his friends thought he was cursed by God. Job's wife was so tired of seeing her husband suffer that she wanted him to forsake God and die to end his suffering. Onlookers may see us go through major tribulations and tell us to forget about God. They would say things like, "If God is real, then He would not have allowed your present trial." In the midst of our difficulties it is natural to get discouraged. Job had an incredibly tough time as he walked through dark valleys. Yet, he stuck with the Lord and continued to seek God even in his weakness. In the midst of turmoil, Job still had the blessing of having a relationship with the Lord. God doesn't waste anything, including our hardships.

Job's friends were not encouragers, they were discouragers. Job could have been jaded by the negativity of his friends. Yet, notice the action Job took toward his friends—he prayed for them. Even in the midst of what we are going through, we still have the privilege to pray for others and retain the joy of the Lord.

God doesn't waste anything, including our hardships.

God is with us through thick and thin, through hardships and heartaches, and He will get us through. He will bring restoration and rejuvenation. God holds us through the most intense tests that we'll ever experience.

The Lord blesses us from above even when dark valleys lie ahead. In difficult seasons, something is added to our spiritual lives—growth. God grows us through those grief-stricken and trial-ridden times. Although things may seem to fall apart, looking back at how God had shaped and refined us makes us appreciate having gone through the trial. Oftentimes we realize how God has used blessings of refinement to chip away our rough edges.

Today, remember that your relationship with God is the biggest blessing in your life. You can endure any and every hardship knowing the Lord allows you to be blessed even through bad circumstances. If you're in a valley, remember that it is temporary. God will use your trying times to tear away from your life anything that is not of Him. He will grow you through those gut-wrenching seasons and you can look back and realize God used the difficulties to help your faith to flourish.

BLESS UNCONDITIONALLY

"Finally, all of you be of one mind, having compassion for one another; love as brothers, be tenderhearted, be courteous; not returning evil for evil or reviling for reviling, but on the contrary blessing, knowing that you were called to this, that you may inherit a blessing." (1 Peter 3:8-9)

It's a blessing to treat people with the same love that God has given us. Without the Lord we would have the wrong heart and attitude toward one another. With the Lord we are able to simply extend the love He's given us to everyone around us. To have compassion on those who are completely against us, we must have the Lord's heart rather than our own.

God sees past the anger and hatred that people have. Instead of seeing people as nuisance, we should see people as in need of Jesus. Instead of seeing people as enemies, we should see people as eternal souls. We are blessed to represent the Lord to those who are lost. People who come against us for our faith are often those who have the hardest hearts toward the Lord. To them we are charged with heralding the gospel. We are called to be kind to those who have hate in their hearts toward God. He is longsuffering and desires that none perish (2 Peter 3:9).

We are blessed and therefore we get to bless others unconditionally.

When we share truth with those who have no desire to know God, we give them a glimpse into God's grace. Many people think they are too far gone for the Lord to ever accept them. God's grace is greater than our biggest sin. As we simply relay the Lord's attributes to them, God can radically work on softening their hearts. May we continue to be examples of the Lord to them. May we never give up in prayer for them. May we realize that there are no impossibilities with the Lord. He can soften the hardest of hearts and He can change those who are fighting against Him. God is powerful. He uses His power not to pounce on people, but to propel the good news to a lost world and to transform those who come to Him.

Today, you have the privilege of reflecting the love of the Lord to a lost world. Even those who see themselves as your enemies can be greatly affected by your love toward them. To bless unconditionally is to realize that even our enemies will end up in eternity. May you have a heart for the lost so that their last day on earth will be their first day with the Lord in heaven. May you rightly reflect the Lord to those who have anger, bitterness and hate toward God. God absolutely loves all—even those with a negative and skeptical attitude toward Him. Portray the love of God through your words, actions and reactions. Demonstrate the love of the Lord so that the lost will see His heart and be blessed to know, believe and accept Him. True love comes from above.

DAY 18

FORGIVEN AND FREE

"Blessed is he whose transgression is forgiven, whose sin is covered." (Psalm 32:1)

What a blessing to be forgiven! One of the things that makes us happy, carefree and blessed is the fact that God holds no transgressions against us. *Transgression* means "to know what is wrong, yet do it anyway." Once we have repented, God does not hold our past failures against us to make us feel guilty or condemned. Our past sins are eradicated and we are vindicated of any wrongdoing. We are blessed because all of those willful sins we engaged in are banished by God. May we remain blessed and not dig up what the Lord has buried. We have no business condemning ourselves for the sins God has forgiven. We can praise God as we remember that Jesus took the sin of humanity upon Himself on the cross of Calvary. No sin or transgression is held against us. God replaces our failures with faith as we are forgiven of all the past wrongs we've committed.

We are blessed because all of those willful sins we engaged in are annihilated.

Our sins are covered by the action that Jesus took on the cross. There is only one solvent for sin, only one way to be forgiven and washed clean. The blood of Christ results in the cleansing of all the sins we have ever engaged in. We are blessed beyond belief that the many mistakes we've made do not lead to complete condemnation or gut-wrenching guilt. Rather, repentance leads to forgive-ness and freedom. We are liberated because of what the Lord has done for us. We can walk confidently in Christ knowing that the sins that were plaguing us, God has put behind Him (Isaiah 38:17). Our cumulative sins are crushed and our deliberate sins are destroyed as we turn from our sin and turn toward God.

Today, remember that true forgiveness from the Father occurs as a result of genuine repentance. If you've confessed and turned away from your sin and turned toward God, you are forgiven and set free from the guilt of your past actions. There is no condemnation for that act that makes you cringe every time it enters your mind. You can breathe with relief as your failures are not held against you. God has forever put the sins of your past behind Him. It's time for you to put those same sins behind you. Walk guilt-free in this God-created world.

GOD'S GRACE

"And of His fullness we have all received, and grace for grace." (John 1:16)

It is a great blessing to receive from the Lord. Jesus told His followers that in order to enter the kingdom, they had to have childlike faith (Mark 10:13-16). Jesus didn't say they had to have childish faith, but childlike faith. A child doesn't argue when someone gives them a present. A child doesn't say, "I don't need that present, I have enough toys and books." A child doesn't say, "You can keep the present you want to give me because I'm saving up my money to buy my own stuff." When a child is given a present, he will joyfully take that present and tear it open! A child simply receives free gifts and is blessed by them. In the same way, we are to simply receive the fullness of God's gifts as little children. The blessings come as we keep it simple. Be blessed by receiving from the Lord and find fulfillment in the spiritual riches He freely offers.

Be blessed by receiving from the Lord.

The grace of God does not run out or fade away. God's grace grinds away the guilt that is associated with thinking we need to work hard to please God. We don't work our way to receive the grace of God. His grace is freely given to us even though we didn't do one thing to deserve it. *Grace upon grace* means that when prior grace runs out, there is more grace waiting for us to receive.

Attempting to work for God's favor will lead to burnout. Striving to receive the grace of God will end in depletion of spiritual fullness. We are fulfilled by simply opening our hands and receiving the overflowing grace of God that He gives to His children. May God's grace go from a concept in our minds to a reality in our hearts.

Today, you will be extremely blessed if you receive and accept the grace of God. You can't work for God's favor, yet it is yours in Christ. Childlike faith means you simply receive from the Lord unconditionally. Grace flows freely from heaven to your heart—it never ends or runs dry. With open hands allow the Lord's grace to fill every facet of your heart and mind. Let God's grace invade your being and what will result is massive blessings from the Maker of heaven and earth.

BLESSING OTHERS

"Give, and it will be given to you: good measure, pressed down, shaken together, and running over will be put into your bosom. For with the same measure that you use, it will be measured back to you." (Luke 6:38)

Giving is a privilege we are blessed to participate in. As we give out what God has given us, we demonstrate a heart that doesn't hoard the Lord's blessings but pours out what God has poured into us. In this verse, Jesus sets us free from the irrational fear of giving too much. The context of the passage is not about giving material resources but about relaying to others those God-given gifts He has blessed us with—forgiveness, freedom, grace, mercy, love and life.

We can never outgive God. As He continually showers us with sweet blessings from above, we are to joyfully and abundantly give to others what God has given us. We are not called to be a burden but a blessing. May we share the Lord and His love and truth with the lost. The greater blessing than receiving from the Lord is giving of the Lord to others.

> **Giving is a privilege we are blessed to participate in.**

We are proclaimers of the gospel which is God's greatest gift to sinful humanity. God has paved a way for a future in heaven. We have the truth that will turn people away from their sin and into a place to accept the Lord. There are countless gifts that God gives us as a result of the gospel—death is defeated, darkness is destroyed, and we have freedom, forgiveness and relief from the grip of sin. We have a relationship with the Lord and a God-given calling to follow. God makes clear our purpose as we simply follow Him. The gospel is groundbreaking in that as God convicts the world, many eyes will be opened to see the true purpose of life. God has and always will be a giver. May we follow His example and give out what God has given us.

Today, remember that you can't outgive God. He wants to bless you in many different ways. But the blessing is not in holding on to those blessings but to share them with those whom God leads you to. Blessing others will help you to keep the right perspective in life. Every good gift was not earned by your hard work; every good gift is from above. Yes, you probably worked hard and accomplished some major feats in life, but remember to give the Gift Giver the glory, honor and praise. Be a blessing by being a giver of God's gifts.

GOD'S WORD

"Blessed is he who reads and those who hear the words of this prophecy, and keep those things which are written in it; for the time is near."
(Revelation 1:3)

We are blessed as a result of reading God's Word. Specifically, we are blessed when we read the book of Revelation. When writing a novel, many professional authors finish the ending before they start writing the beginning. Knowing the outcome in the future will help us have victory in the present. In Revelation we know who wins. God has the victory. The Lord takes out the dark foes and spiritual enemies that are against us. In reading Revelation, we are blessed because it gives us a picture of how to live life now. What a complete blessing to be walking with the Lord in this life at this moment in time. The Lord leads us to triumph through the greatest and deepest trials. We depend on Him through the most intense difficulties.

Prophecy is important because what God has said will come to pass. So as we read His future promises, we see that the future is bright for the believer. The last book of the Bible gives us a glimpse of heaven. There will be no more death, sorrow, crying or pain (Revelation 21:4). Be blessed by reading this book.

What a complete blessing to be walking with the Lord in this life.

Life is like a vapor (James 4:14). Knowing we have limited time will cause us to live with a sense of urgency. As believers we should care more about quality than quantity. It's not about how long we live on this earth; it's about how well we live for the Lord while we are on this earth. Time is a precious commodity and we want to make this one life count for Christ. Knowing time is short will help us realign our priorities and run our race well. We are not guaranteed tomorrow. While we still have breath in our lungs and passion in our heart for the Lord, we have the blessed responsibility to share the gospel with this world. All the events in Revelation haven't yet come to pass because there are still more people who need to be saved. May we step out of our inhibited selves and share God's glorious truth with others.

Today, find hope and blessing in reading the book of Revelation. Know that the Lord is in control and ultimately has the victory. You are on the right side of the fight for the faith. You are saved from eternal judgment and can look forward to being with the Lord in eternity. What a blessing.

ETERNAL OUTLOOK

"Blessed are the poor in spirit, for theirs is the kingdom of heaven." (Matthew 5:3)

The word *blessed* describes a joy that is palpable and self-contained. *Blessed* means contentment in spite of our outward circumstances. Being poor in spirit means that a believer has the right view of their spiritual state without the Lord. Without believing in and accepting the Lord Jesus Christ, we are spiritually bankrupt. Without God we are the poorest people. Jesus started the Beatitudes with being poor in spirit because that is the place to start with God. We need to have a right view of our lives. We are blessed in knowing that we can't grow, thrive or flourish spiritually without the Lord, the Faith Giver. Those who think they can stand without the Lord will fall. Those who think they can make it through life without the Lord will fail. When we peer into our own wicked hearts (Jeremiah 17:9), it shows us our desperate need for Him, and it leads to a hunger and thirst after Him. This is a blessed state to be in as it leads to total dependency upon the Holy Spirit to fill and fulfill us.

Without God we are the poorest people.

Being poor in spirit is the prerequisite for receiving the kingdom of heaven. When our hearts are depleted of self-sufficiency, we are in a state of humility and are primed to receive the Lord. Every effective kingdom builder can have the most impact when they have a heart of humility. Clinging to the Lord for dear life is the best action we can take knowing we cannot gain any ground without God. God is who gives us all we need to be refined and restored. He resuscitates us spiritually. He wakes us up and sets us on the path that leads to paradise. He meets us at our most destitute state and douses us with the Holy Spirit so we can get up and go forward. The kingdom of God is our future as long as we give up the fight and let the Lord fight our battles (Luke 22:32). May we raise our hands in surrender realizing that God does the work as we empty us of ourselves. Only then can we be fully dependent upon the One who guides every step we take.

Today, remember that you are empty without an eternal outlook. You can do nothing without the Holy Spirit's leading. When you realize the state of your heart without the Lord, the result will be an intense reliance upon Him. The kingdom awaits those who have hearts of humility. When you are poor in spirit, you become rich in kingdom resources. The emptiness and apathy will turn into a fullness and excitement that will grow your spiritual life like nothing else.

DAY 23

BE COMFORTED

"Blessed are those who mourn, for they shall be comforted." (Matthew 5:4)

Mourning is the avenue to see our almighty God move in our lives. The Greek word for *mourning* means "a deep, intense, and sorrowful grieving." It means grief as if someone has died. One would wonder how blessings can emanate from mourning. Jesus is speaking about our fallen state as human beings. We are all sinners in need of the Savior. To have a right view of our sinful hearts is to be grieved over sin and the actions that we've taken in life. We mourn because of the low and needy state that we are in without the Lord. Believers who don't mourn over sin will be complacent toward it. They may be in self-denial thinking that they are in line with the Lord when they are not. The reality is we are all in a desperate state since sin is destructive and dangerous. When we see the effects of sin as harmful, we'll be quick to repent and get back on track.

> Believers who don't mourn over sin may be complacent toward it.

Mourning is the precursor to repentance. When we are aware of our sin, we repent and get right with God. To repent means to have a change of mind and a change of direction. To repent means to turn from sin toward God. When we know the state of our hearts, it leads to mourning, which leads to repentance, which results in comfort. None of us are anywhere close to perfect. None of us have it all together. None of us have conquered sin completely. Jesus has conquered sin on the cross and makes intercession for us. He gives us strength daily to resist temptation. As we fall short of God's glory, we mourn over the sin we commit. Yet we can find complete comfort in the fact that we *can* actually repent. God has made a way through repentance to stay close to Him and not alienate ourselves from a relationship with Him. A sign of Christian maturity is not perfection but being quick to repent when we fail.

Today, please realize the destructiveness of sin, and turn from it. Be quick to repent when you drift off your God-given path. Be comforted by the fact that the Lord has made a way for you to be restored and fully forgiven. Know that as you sorrow over your own sin, it will lead to repentance, which will lead to relief of any and all guilt. The perfect heart to have toward God is one that mourns over your sin realizing that you desperately need the Lord.

DAY 24

SPIRITUALLY STRONG

"Blessed are the meek, for they shall inherit the earth." (Matthew 5:5)

Meekness means strength under control. Meekness does not mean abundant weakness. Meekness means to be submissive under an authority figure. It has to do with adhering to God's Word, gaining strength from Him and moving forward with the Lord's strength. The meek person will get angry and channel that anger to strength in order to stand up for what they believe in. The meek person may get angry, but not sin (Ephesians 4:26). The meek person will stand up and fight for their faith, but not become belligerent or out of control. The meek person will handle confrontation in a godly way instead of backing down out of the way.

It is a blessing to be meek for it signifies that we are wholly and completely depending upon the Lord for everything we need. To have this confidence is to know and believe that God watches out for us, protects us and fills us with strength to fulfill our calling. It means we have strength that is in line with God's will. We don't let that strength be unchecked or out of control. We don't back down, but we press on knowing the Lord will get us through everything that we face.

> The meek person will stand up and fight for their faith, but not become belligerent or out of control.

From God's perspective, being meek is a blessing that will result in inheriting the earth. God will not allow the meek to be pushed around, get the short end of the stick, or be doormats to be walked on. Rather they are brave believers who adhere to their almighty God, who stand up for the faith, and are completely within God's will. When we are meek, we have strength from God, not to wield that strength to bring others down but to raise up the Lord's name.

Today, as God gives you strength and the ability to keep that strength under control, live for what matters. You are spiritually strong because of the integration of the Holy Spirit into your very life. God will lift you up, set you on His path and give you vigor and passion to fulfill His purposes. Look up and realize God's power flowing through you to deal with any and every situation.

DAY 25

FILL YOUR SOUL

"Blessed are those who hunger and thirst for righteousness, for they shall be filled." (Matthew 5:6)

The more we seek the Lord, the more our hunger grows for the Lord. We hunger for many things in this world that do not lead to a happy and fulfilled life. We attempt to fill ourselves by achieving success, status, money, or fame. As fallen human beings, we tend to feed off of things that don't come close to fulfilling our soul and we're left wanting and striving for satisfaction. In reality, the things that fill the heart are not outward at all. As food fills the longing in our stomach, the spiritual fills the longing in our soul. When we seek the Lord, a passion ignites in us that sets our heart aflame to pursue the Lord. We begin to be driven to seek God more and more. Our affections begin to point toward the things of the Lord and we long to know Jesus that much more. Like a good meal that we love and desire often, the things of God become what we fall in love with and constantly long for. Seeking the Lord's righteousness becomes the priority and point of life.

As we simply and consistently follow the Lord, we will go from starving to satisfied, hungry to healthy, fatigued to full.

The Lord satisfies the soul that is hungry and thirsty for righteousness. When we are hungering and thirsting for righteousness, we are not simultaneously hungering and thirsting for worldly pleasures. We desire more of the Lord and we put aside selfish living. To be righteous means to be right before the Lord, to be surrendered to Him, focusing on spiritual matters rather than earthly drama.

Jesus blesses us with access to the living water that satisfies the thirst that only He can fulfill. It feels good to be filled. Soul satisfaction stems from seeking the Savior on a regular basis. The way to satiate our soul is to fill it with more of God. John the Baptist said something profound in the midst of a conflict that was going on between his disciples and the Jews. He said, "He must increase, but I must decrease" (John 3:30).

Today, fill your soul with the spiritual, not the carnal. You will be blessed from above as you keep focused on the Father. As you passionately pursue the Lord, He will crowd out any earthly desires that will only keep your heart and soul unfulfilled. The more you seek Jesus, the more you will desire to walk rightly in this world with His strength. Fill your soul with spiritual things that satisfy. What a blessing to be a believer and feed of the Lord's faithfulness.

EXTEND MERCY

"Blessed are the merciful, for they shall obtain mercy." (Matthew 5:7)

God has truly blessed us by not giving us what we deserve. Being born into spiritual poverty, we deserved death, darkness and destruction. We could not earn mercy, nor could we strive for mercy. Because of God's great mercy upon those who call upon Him, we are saved from spiritual separation from the Lord. We cannot achieve a closeness to the Lord without the mercy of God. His mercy was demonstrated on the cross of Calvary two thousand years ago. We desperately need God's mercy in order to be forgiven and walk rightly with Him. God's mercy is amazing. We don't deserve to have a place prepared for us in heaven; yet Jesus died so we can enter into a relationship with Him and have a future home in heaven. Realizing the wonderful mercy of God, we are forever changed and eternally grateful.

God has truly blessed us by not giving us what we deserve.

Understanding the mercy of God helps us to extend mercy to those who are in need and suffering. Extending mercy means we can bless others without expecting anything in return. There are many ways we can show and demonstrate God's mercy. Mercy is not something that is popular in our society today.

People ask questions like, *Why would we show mercy to our enemies? Why would we show mercy to those who don't deserve to be forgiven? Why should we show mercy to those who are poor and are not working for their money? Why should we show mercy to the sinner who doesn't care about the souls of others?* The answer is because God showed mercy to us. It's a blessing to readily give out what God has freely given to us.

Today, be merciful to those who don't deserve it. You are blessed because God does not give you what you deserve. You are blessed because the Lord's love is the reason why He relays mercy to you every single day. Embrace God's mercy, and then extend mercy to those who are broken and in desperate need of the Lord.

DAY 27

SEEING GOD

"Blessed are the pure in heart, for they shall see God." (Matthew 5:8)

An undivided heart that's bent on the Lord results in a blessed life. The word *pure* in this verse means "honest with God; purposing in one's heart to fully follow the Lord Jesus." It means walking a straight path in line with the Lord's ways, seeking after God's heart rather than one's own desires. To be pure in heart has to do with commitment and devotion.

It's such a blessing to commit our ways to the Lord and devote our every day to Him. The Lord isn't concerned with how we look on the outside, the Lord looks at the heart. So the question becomes, *Is our heart fully following the Lord?* The answer will be clear when we seek God and ask Him to expose those areas in us that are not of Him. Being pure doesn't mean we are perfect or sinless. Being pure means we sin less because we want to follow God more. We are set apart to live our lives in ultimate surrender to Him.

> An undivided heart that's bent on the Lord results in a blessed life.

To be pure in heart is to have intimate connection with the Lord—it's the most amazing reward ever. Sin, on the other hand, results in a distant and disconnected relationship with God. Sin blinds us and causes our vision of the Lord to be blurred. If we live partly for the Lord and partly for the world, we will not enjoy that closeness and nearness to God that He so desires with us. Sin truly impedes our progress in growing spiritually and thriving in our relationship with God. But the pure in heart will see God in His Word, in creation, and in every situation. The pure in heart can walk with God unhindered and unobstructed.

Today, you have the privilege of living with a pure heart before God. True happiness stems from staying closely connected to the Lord and devoting your whole heart to following Him. Purpose in your heart to daily walk with the Lord, forsaking sin and connecting with Him. As you live to please the Lord, who provides all that you need, you will have joy that is full and blessings that bring true contentment. Seeing God is the glorious future for those who live, not with a perfect heart, but with a pure heart.

PEACE THAT LASTS

"Blessed are the peacemakers, for they shall be called sons of God." (Matthew 5:9)

It is a blessing to bring about peace. This verse speaks about those who actively do their part as believers to portray and reflect peace in this world. Those who bring about peace overcome evil with good.

One avenue to accomplish making peace is through spreading the gospel message. This is the message that sinful man, who has no peace apart from God, can connect with the holy God through Christ. People attempt to find peace in locations, situations and circumstances. What many people don't realize is that true peace comes from our relationship with the Lord. His peace is everlasting and we get to tell that truth to this world that is full of turmoil and chaos. Being a peacemaker is to see a fire of conflict and to put out that fire with the Lord's help. That is the picture of a peacemaker. Oftentimes the fire is caused by the enemy, the world, or the flesh. These three opposing forces attempt to eradicate any peace that we have, yet God is stronger, and He is the source of peace.

Those who bring about peace overcome evil with good.

Being a peacemaker yields the reward of being a child of God. When we desire for others to have true peace through the gospel, we are in line with God's heart for the lost. As a child of God we get to enjoy peace in our hearts and lives despite our circumstances or location. We are blessed to know the peace of Jesus, which is not a fleeting worldly peace but a peace that never perishes (John 14:27). What a privilege and blessing that God has given us.

Today, you have the opportunity to share the gospel message that brings connection between sinful man and a holy God. You have the privilege to see people come to Christ and finally have peace that lasts. You are a child of God, and this is precisely why you have peace through the problems you face in your life. Don't forget that the peace of God is there for the taking every single day. Extend His peace to people who truly need it.

COUNT IT A BLESSING

"Blessed are those who are persecuted for righteousness' sake, for theirs is the kingdom of heaven." (Matthew 5:10)

To be persecuted for the name of Jesus is actually a privilege. We never pray for problems or persecutions to arise, but as we live wholehearted lives for the Lord, there will be opposition. Of course, there are varying degrees of persecution depending upon where we live in this world. To experience pushback for living a sold out life for Christ is a blessing. It demonstrates that we are courageous in carrying out the Great Commission. Think about those people in the Bible who were driven to live for the Lord. They went through intense trials and opposition that most of us will never face. They were passionate and they stayed passionate even as they faced fiery trials and condemnation. Living for righteousness can lead to persecution, but it demonstrates we are actually living for the Lord and are not ashamed of the gospel (Romans 1:16).

To experience pushback for living a sold out life for Christ is a blessing.

To live for the Lord is a huge blessing that reaps an awe-inspiring benefit—heaven. Heaven is filled with those who have heralded the gospel in the face of opposition. As we live for the Lord in this short life that we've been given, we have a blessed future to look forward to. What we do on this earth will ultimately affect our future in eternity. May we give our whole selves to the work of God's kingdom. May we not back down or let intimidation shut up the truth that is burning in our bones waiting to be released. May we live in such a way that people see the conviction in which we live and can't help but be attracted to the message of grace. May we be filled with the Spirit and live lives that are full of courage and beaming with boldness. May we move forward despite makeshift roadblocks that opposers may attempt to put in our way. May we never stop but rather continue to invest in the things of the Lord.

Today, don't let possible worldly repercussions stop you from sharing the story of redemption. Keep speaking boldly in the name of Jesus. Count it a blessing if you face opposition for telling truth. It simply means you are propelling the gospel and not backing down. Experiencing pushback means you are bringing the gospel to this world that is growing darker and darker by the day. Shine that light!

DAY 30

BE JOYFUL

"Blessed are you when they revile and persecute you, and say all kinds of evil against you falsely for My sake. Rejoice and be exceedingly glad, for great is your reward in heaven, for so they persecuted the prophets who were before you." (Matthew 5:11-12)

We can rejoice when we are hated for our faith. Persecution isn't just physical, it's verbal as well. Some people are so against the faith they will spew insults in our direction. For us, the faith is real, personal, and life-changing, but those who hate the faith will play dirty and do all they can to discredit truth. Instead of leaving our faith alone and living life peacefully with us, they intolerantly attempt to make us feel bad for believing.

Think about the ministry of Jesus. He was ridiculed, mocked, insulted and verbally torn down by those who were against Him. When unbelievers lie because of their hatred toward our faith, may we answer them with the Lord's love. May we stay determined to share the gospel with them and may we let nothing deter us from the truth that transforms the hardest of hearts.

For us, the faith is real, personal, and life changing.

Rejoicing should be the result of being verbally attacked. This seems strange at first, until we realize that the prophets who were before us poured out their lives for the Lord and were denounced for their boldness. The word *rejoicing* in this verse can be translated "leaping for joy." How can we have joy when people mock what we know is true? How can we have joy when others talk down to us because of our faith? We can have joy in the midst of persecution because our reward is not earthly; it's eternal. God blesses those who live unashamedly for Him. May we never lose heart as we do good for God in this life. May our countenance be lifted when someone becomes livid toward us because of God.

We will face opposition in many different ways, but we rejoice because we are building up our treasure in heaven. Let's keep our eyes fixed on heaven—we are not working for earthly rewards; we are serving God for eternal dividends. Keep building the kingdom and serving the Lord despite opposition. It pleases God when we live to build His kingdom in heaven and not our own little kingdoms on earth.

Today, rejoice when people revile you. Be joyful when haters come against you. Respond to their hate with love. When you experience pushback for sharing truth, let it be an indicator that you are living a life poured out for Christ. Let it solidify and establish your faith that much more because God truly blesses those who live boldly for Him.

DAY 31

BEAUTIFUL BLESSINGS

"The LORD bless you and keep you; the LORD make His face shine on you and be gracious to you; the LORD turn His face toward you and give you peace." (Numbers 6:24-26 NIV)

This verse is called the Aaronic blessing. It's a blessing that the Lord *turns His face* toward us. This means He pays attention to us. How amazing that God favors us and pays attention to us! It simply shows that God absolutely loves to bless His people. It also demonstrates that all blessings come from the Lord. God's blessings are more than comfort, riches and happiness. God's blessings are bestowed upon us even as we are going through burdensome times. During the storms of life, God keeps us, gives us life, sustains us, protects us, and gives us rest.

What a blessing that God's face *shines* upon us. This means that God is pleased with us, not because of who we are but because of who we are in Him. To think that God is well pleased with us as we follow Him is a huge blessing. God is gracious to us as well. He gives us what we don't deserve. We don't deserve His grace, yet because we are saved His favor is upon us! What a blessing to worship and serve God who thinks of us, loves us, favors us, and blesses us. There is nothing better than living our lives for the Lord. Nothing.

It's a blessing to be kept by our God.

The Lord wants to bless you. In these verses the word *you* is used six times. This is significant because it indicates that God wants to bless His children. Many times we think God wants to bless everyone else except for us. That's the wrong way of thinking. God wants to bless every single one of His children. Walking in God's will is how we enter into the blessings of God. As we daily seek the Lord, He will daily bless us! May we always remember that God has our best interests in mind, and He will lead us down the path where He can use us the most. God wants to use our lives to capacity as long as we have life on this earth. As we consistently serve Him, we will be blessed by being radically used by God in this land.

Today, know that God wants to bless you. Know that God favors you. Know that God loves you. Know that there are abundant blessings in simply following the Lord. You have been so blessed by God in the past. You are so blessed by God in the present. If that's not enough, God wants to bless you in the future. You are living in God's beautiful blessings. Don't forget that the blessings of God are not because of what you did or the work that you have accomplished. The blessings of God flow down from heaven because of how good God is. I pray you believe this with all your heart. You are blessed because of God's massive love for you. Revel in that. Rest in that. Be refreshed that the Lord of the universe created you out of pure love. May these truths bring a sure hope to your heart and a huge smile on your face. God bless you!

CONCLUSION

"Blessed are the people who know the joyful sound! They walk, O LORD, in the light of Your countenance." (Psalm 89:15)

As believers living in this world at this point in time, we are incredibly blessed. God has created us, sustained us, and saved us. The Lord gives us wisdom, strength, joy, love, and everything that pertains to life and godliness (2 Peter 1:3). The Lord makes life clear. God leads us where we are supposed to go and what we are to do when we get there. Acts 2:42 gives us a clear view of the early church activities that we are blessed to participate in. He has given us His Word to lead us and speak to us. He has given us the avenue of prayer to communicate with Him and grow in our relationship with Him. He has given us the blessing of fellowship to connect with other like minded believers so as to build one another up. We get to take communion to always remember what Jesus went through for our freedom. What a blessing to be a believer.

I hope and pray that this small devotional reminds you of the blessings of the Lord upon your life. I could write many more books about how blessed you are as a believer. I pray that you would realize daily how you can have pure joy by simply being a believer. God loves you so much and He is with you always. The Lord cares what you go through, no matter what it is. He wants to meet you where you are at in your life. Let Him in and surrender completely to His leading and you'll fully enter into the plan that He has for you. I pray that as you live your life for God, you will be able to simply relay the blessings you have to others. Let the fact that you are saved instill in you a joy that is infectious.

You are blessed beyond measure. You are blessed forever. You are blessed even through bad times. You are blessed because you believe and follow the God who created the universe and communicates with you. Soak that truth in. Believe that He has blessed you and wants to continue to bless you abundantly. Bless Him in return by living a life that is on fire for Him. It's all worth it.

www.ingramcontent.com/pod-product-compliance
Lightning Source LLC
Chambersburg PA
CBHW072027060426
42449CB00035B/2924